Little People, **BIG DREAMS**™

PRINCESS DIANA

Written by
Maria Isabel Sánchez Vegara

Illustrated by
Archita Khosla

Frances Lincoln
Children's Books

Once upon a time, a girl called Diana was born into a noble British family. She was the third daughter, and not the son and heir that her parents had hoped for. Still, she was such a breath of joy that she became the apple of her father's eye.

When Diana was seven, her parents divorced. From that day on, the children lived only with their father, and Diana did her best to take care of her younger brother, Charles. Her hugs were filled with the love that a kid needs to grow.

Two years later Diana was sent to a boarding school far away from home. She was a talented pianist and ballerina, and although she didn't excel as a student, her kindness earned her a prize for being the most caring girl in school.

She was sharing an apartment with three good friends and working at a preschool when she caught the eye of Prince Charles—the heir to the British throne.

She soon realized that
she had fallen in love!

On the day they were married, thousands of people waited to see the bride, and 750 million people worldwide watched the ceremony on television.

But Diana kept a little secret for herself under her heels:
a hidden "C" and "D" for Charles and Diana.

It wasn't just the prince who seemed to have fallen in love with her, but the whole country. Wherever the couple went for their royal duties, thousands of waving hands welcomed them both.

Still, Diana captivated people the most
with her freshness and charm.

But even though her life seemed to be taken from the pages of a fairy tale, Diana soon realized that the prince's heart belonged to someone else. She fell into a deep sadness. Over time, that sadness grew into an eating disorder called bulimia.

Whenever she felt alone, she felt better by eating all the treats she could find in the royal kitchens. But that sweet feeling of comfort didn't last long. Once it was gone, she would try to get rid of all the food she had eaten by making herself throw up.

It took her time to seek help, learn to love herself, and stop hurting her body. But once she did, she felt better than ever. She was one of the first famous people to speak up about her struggle with bulimia, helping others to confront it, too.

Diana blossomed into an independent princess. She knew that the best way to serve the Crown was by being a caring mother for her children, William and Harry.

So despite her royal duties, she always found time to be with them.

Whatever she did was in the news, and she used that fame to help others. By hugging patients with AIDS, she showed that the condition doesn't make people dangerous to know.

And she promoted the removal of landmines
by visiting fields once full of them.

When Diana and Charles announced their divorce,
she lost the title of "Her Royal Highness."

Still, she kept charming people with her own kind of magic and shining a light on important causes, from mental-health issues to animal rights.

And little Diana never regretted leaving the palace
to follow her own path: the path of a true princess
who—by opening herself up to others—became
a queen in people's hearts.

PRINCESS DIANA

(Born 1961 – Died 1997)

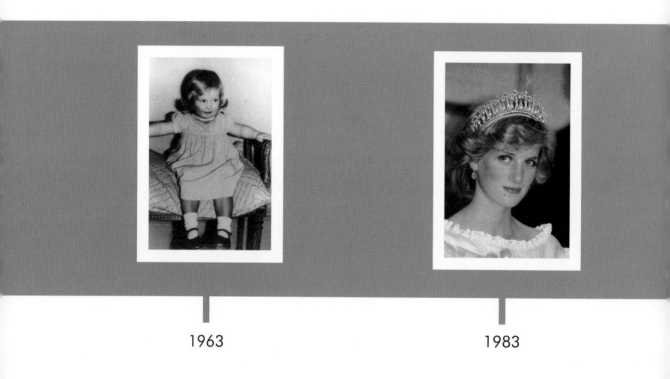

1963

1983

Diana Spencer was the youngest daughter of Viscount Althorp and his wife, Frances. After her parents divorced when she was seven, she and her siblings lived with their father. Her caring nature was noticed by many growing up, and after school she moved to London and became a preschool teacher's assistant. Diana met Prince Charles when she was a teenager, and as adults their friendship blossomed into romance. When the couple married on July 29, 1981, the ceremony was televised and watched by millions around the world! Diana rapidly became known for her grace and elegance. She used her status to raise awareness for numerous charitable causes such as the National AIDS Trust, the HALO Trust—which works to remove landmines—and many more. Her stylish hair and wardrobe made her a trendsetter and,

1986   1997

in the eyes of the public, she was the perfect princess. But Diana struggled with depression, low self-esteem, eating disorders, and strain from constant media attention. Her marriage to Prince Charles ended and the couple formally separated in 1992. After her divorce, Diana maintained her public profile. She took her sons Prince William and Prince Harry with her to hospitals, homeless shelters, and orphanages to show them a world outside of royal privilege. With professional help, she learned to love herself and she was one of the first celebrities to speak up about the effects of bulimia. Sadly, Diana was killed in a car accident in 1997 at age 36. The world was utterly stunned to lose her so suddenly. An icon of love, compassion, and charity, Diana will always be the "People's Princess."

Want to find out more about **Princess Diana?**

Have a read of this great book:

The Story of Princess Diana by Jenna Grodzicki

If you're in London, England, you can visit the statue of Princess Diana
in the Sunken Garden at Kensington Palace.

Brimming with creative inspiration, how-to
projects, and useful information to enrich your
everyday life, quarto.com is a favourite destination
for those pursuing their interests and passions.

Text © 2023 Maria Isabel Sánchez Vegara. Illustrations © 2023 Archita Khosla.
"Little People, BIG DREAMS" and "Pequeña & Grande" are trademarks of
Alba Editorial S.L.U. and/or Beautifool Couple S.L.
First Published in the USA in 2023 by Frances Lincoln Children's Books, an imprint of The Quarto Group.
Quarto Boston North Shore, 100 Cummings Center, Suite 265D, Beverly, MA 01915, USA
Tel: +1 978-282-9590, Fax: +1 978-283-2742, www.Quarto.com

This book is not authorized, licenced, or approved by the estate of Princess Diana.
Any faults are the publisher's, who will be happy to rectify for future printings.
A catalogue record for this book is available from the Library of Congress.
ISBN 978-0-7112-8307-7
Set in Futura BT.

Published by Peter Marley • Designed by Sasha Moxon
Commissioned by Lucy Menzies • Edited by Lucy Menzies and Rachel Robinson
Production by Nikki Ingram
Manufactured in Guangdong, China CC102022
1 3 5 7 9 8 6 4 2

Photographic acknowledgements (pages 28-29, from left to right): 1. 1st July 1963: Lady Diana Frances Spencer (1961 - 1997),
later Princess of Wales, aged 2, at Park House, Sandringham, Norfolk. © Keystone/Stringer via Getty Images. 2. AUCKLAND, NEW
ZEALAND - APRIL 29: Diana, Princess of Wales, wearing a cream satin dress by Gina Fratini with the Queen Mary Cambridge Lover's
Knot Tiara and diamond earrings attends a banquet on April 29, 1983 in Auckland, New Zealand. © Anwar Hussein via Getty
Images. 3. Diana, Princess of Wales (1961 - 1997) during a trip to Canada, May 1986. © Georges De Keerle via Getty Images. 4.
HUAMBO, ANGOLA - JANUARY 15: Diana, Princess of Wales, walks with body armour and a visor on the minefields during a visit to
Huambo, Angola on January 15, 1997. © Anwar Hussein Collection via Getty Images.

Collect the *Little People*, **BIG DREAMS**™ series:

FRIDA KAHLO 	**COCO CHANEL**	**MAYA ANGELOU**	**AMELIA EARHART**	**AGATHA CHRISTIE**	**MARIE CURIE**	**ROSA PARKS**	**AUDREY HEPBURN**
EMMELINE PANKHURST	**ELLA FITZGERALD**	**ADA LOVELACE**	**JANE AUSTEN**	**GEORGIA O'KEEFFE**	**HARRIET TUBMAN**	**ANNE FRANK**	**MOTHER TERESA** 
JOSEPHINE BAKER 	**L. M. MONTGOMERY**	**JANE GOODALL**	**SIMONE DE BEAUVOIR**	**MUHAMMAD ALI**	**STEPHEN HAWKING**	**MARIA MONTESSORI**	**VIVIENNE WESTWOOD**
MAHATMA GANDHI 	**DAVID BOWIE**	**WILMA RUDOLPH**	**DOLLY PARTON**	**BRUCE LEE**	**RUDOLF NUREYEV** 	**ZAHA HADID** 	**MARY SHELLEY**
MARTIN LUTHER KING JR.	**DAVID ATTENBOROUGH**	**ASTRID LINDGREN**	**EVONNE GOOLAGONG**	**BOB DYLAN** 	**ALAN TURING** 	**BILLIE JEAN KING**	**GRETA THUNBERG**
JESSE OWENS	**JEAN-MICHEL BASQUIAT** 	**ARETHA FRANKLIN**	**CORAZON AQUINO** 	**PELÉ**	**ERNEST SHACKLETON** 	**STEVE JOBS** 	**AYRTON SENNA** 
LOUISE BOURGEOIS	**ELTON JOHN** 	**JOHN LENNON**	**PRINCE**	**CHARLES DARWIN**	**CAPTAIN TOM MOORE**	**HANS CHRISTIAN ANDERSEN**	**STEVIE WONDER**

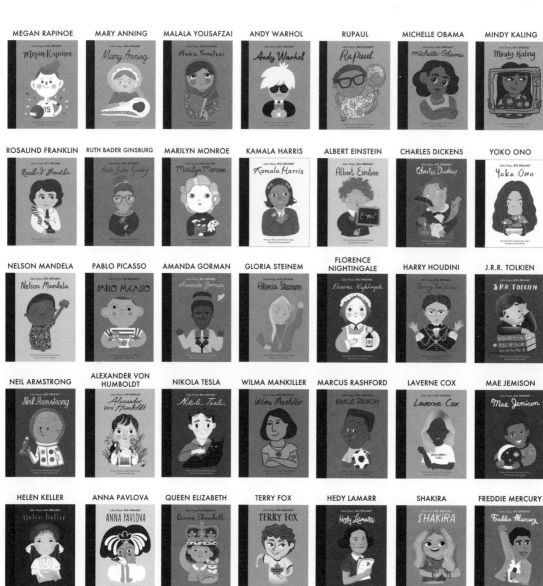

MEGAN RAPINOE · MARY ANNING · MALALA YOUSAFZAI · ANDY WARHOL · RUPAUL · MICHELLE OBAMA · MINDY KALING · IRIS APFEL

ROSALIND FRANKLIN · RUTH BADER GINSBURG · MARILYN MONROE · KAMALA HARRIS · ALBERT EINSTEIN · CHARLES DICKENS · YOKO ONO · MICHAEL JORDAN

NELSON MANDELA · PABLO PICASSO · AMANDA GORMAN · GLORIA STEINEM · FLORENCE NIGHTINGALE · HARRY HOUDINI · J.R.R. TOLKIEN · ELVIS PRESLEY

NEIL ARMSTRONG · ALEXANDER VON HUMBOLDT · NIKOLA TESLA · WILMA MANKILLER · MARCUS RASHFORD · LAVERNE COX · MAE JEMISON · DWAYNE JOHNSON

HELEN KELLER · ANNA PAVLOVA · QUEEN ELIZABETH · TERRY FOX · HEDY LAMARR · SHAKIRA · FREDDIE MERCURY · LEWIS HAMILTON

LOUIS PASTEUR

PRINCESS DIANA

ACTIVITY BOOKS

STICKER ACTIVITY BOOK

COLORING BOOK

LITTLE ME, BIG DREAMS JOURNAL

Discover more about the series at www.littlepeoplebigdreams.com